Managing the Modern Languages Classroom

Amanda Flint
County Consultant (Languages), Surrey Education Services

Anna Lise Gordon
Modern Foreign Languages Consultant

ALL/MGP

ASSOCIATION for LANGUAGE LEARNING

Mary Glasgow Publications

The authors and publishe[illegible] would like to thank Michèle Deane, ALL consultant, for collating comments on [illegible]he manuscript on behalf of ALL.

Designed by Janet McCallu[illegible]
Illustrations by Mike K[illegible]arnyckyj
Typeset by Tech-Se[illegible]eshead, Tyne & Wear
Printed and bou[illegible] in Great Britain

An imprint of Stanley Thornes (Publishers) Ltd.
Ellenborough House
Wellington Street
CHELTENHAM
GL50 1YD

Reprinted 1994

A catalogue record for this publication is available from the British Library.

ISBN ~~0-85234-509-8~~

Books in the *Concepts* series:

Concepts 1 Using the Target Language by Carol Macdonald
Concepts 2 Appraisal for Language Teachers by Michael Pennington
Concepts 3 Managing the Modern Languages Classroom by Amanda Flint and Anna Lise Gordon
Concepts 4 Teaching and Learning Grammar by Alison Taylor
Concepts 5 Working with your Student Teacher by Sarah Fletcher and Mike Calvert
Concepts 6 Being a Head of Department by Amanda Flint and Anna Lise Gordon

Contents

Introduction

From the President of ALL

The *Concepts* series marks a new phase in the activities of the Association for Language Learning. I am confident that the series will be welcomed as a noteworthy addition to the services of the Association offered to its existing members and it should attract others to take up membership. The combination of the publishing expertise of Mary Glasgow Publications with the practical and professional knowledge of ALL will guarantee that our books meet the needs of practising teachers across the various educational sections and in all parts of the UK. It is our intention that the books will provide positive and constructive guidance for the classroom practitioner. There are many new challenges facing the profession and we hope that this series will come to be viewed as a valuable source of professional support. The busy working life of teachers makes it essential for the texts to be accessible and direct. We hope you, the readers, will find both realism and inspiration within the pages of this book and in the other books in the *Concepts* series.

Bob Powell
ALL President 1991–94

About this book

Perhaps you have just started teaching or have recently restarted?
Perhaps you have been in the profession for some years and feel it is time to look afresh at your teaching?
Perhaps you are interested in classroom management and in what the National Curriculum means for your teaching?
Perhaps you've just had a bad lesson and want some ideas?
Or perhaps someone – a colleague or an inspector – is coming in to see you teach?
Whatever your personal starting point, classroom management is something for all teachers to consider at all points in their career.

Classroom management

The term 'classroom management' borrows the notion of management from the business world. It is a neat term, implying a clear code of practice. But the reference to the classroom is actually a distraction. Classroom management is really about how you teach a lesson, how you manage your pupils and – more exactly – how you manage their learning.

Managing learning, then, is the vital issue. It is because we are dealing with pupils' learning – a vast and complex area – that successful classroom management is far from easy. There is no magic recipe; we all bring our own personal qualities and skills to our work with our pupils.

In the context of the changes brought about by the National Curriculum, this book outlines some practical ideas and activities for developing your own classroom management. This process of development may take a little time and there is never very much spare time in a school. But time spent developing good practice may save some of the time which might otherwise be spent sorting out difficulties later on.

Certain themes recur in this book:

- The Statutory Orders and Non-statutory Guidance for Modern Foreign Languages provide our professional starting point. Many of the activities in this book are cross-referenced to the Attainment Targets (AT) and the *Programme of Study Part 1* (PoS).
- Now that all pupils are entitled to a foreign language experience, the issue of access is particularly important. What we think we're teaching is not necessarily what pupils end up learning. Successful classroom management involves taking into account the needs of each pupil, the design of the tasks and the learning environment. These are key aspects of a teacher's work, leading towards effective differentiation. It is this differentiation which gives all pupils access to the curriculum.
- Successful classroom management involves a series of processes:
  - reviewing your current practice
  - planning
  - preparing
  - teaching the lesson
  - assessing pupils' work
  - evaluating your own work.
- Classroom management is an important issue not only for you as an individual teacher but also for your department. Working collaboratively on aspects of classroom management helps to ensure departmental consistency by giving all pupils a similar range of learning experiences but it also provides the most supportive way of developing your own practice. This is why this book includes several staff development activities. Where examples are included, these are not intended as models to be copied but rather as discussion points for you as a department to compare with examples from your own teaching.

1 Classroom management: getting it in perspective

The purpose of this chapter is to present a process of audit and planning for you to use when reviewing your own practice.

- What should I be doing?
- What am I doing?
- What do I want to do next? And how?
- How will I know if I have been successful?

What should I be doing?

This used to be a difficult question, as we could always say it was a matter of personal opinion. We now have a statutory National Curriculum and the ringbinder gives clear indications of those aspects of classroom management required to deliver this curriculum. Our National Curriculum document has two main sections:

- the Attainment Targets which provide a focus for assessment (see Chapter 7), and
- the *Programme of Study* which deals with the skills, processes, content and contexts for learning.

Focusing on learning opportunities, the *Programme of Study* should be reflected in our teaching and, as such, should be constantly reviewed.

Using the target language as the main means of learning

The second main section of the ringbinder gives the general requirements for the *Programme of Study* in languages. Part 1 *Learning and using the target language* gives six broad skill areas.

Pupils must learn to:

- communicate in the target language
- understand and respond
- develop language learning skills and awareness of language
- develop cultural awareness
- develop the ability to work with others
- develop the ability to work independently.

All this in the target language!

In other words, this is a pupil-centred curriculum. It is not enough for the teacher to use the target language and for the pupils to be immersed in it; pupils must actively use the language themselves.

The implication for classroom management is that teachers need strategies to ensure a high level of active pupil use of the foreign language, as well as strategies to ensure their own use of the target language for all aspects of the lesson. (The first book in the *Concepts* series of handbooks for language teachers – *Using the Target Language* – offers practical suggestions for such strategies. See the booklist on page 29.)

The *Programme of Study Part 1* gives many hints about classroom management. It describes all those activities which pupils should have 'regular opportunities' to do; it is the teacher who must plan to provide those opportunities for learning within the context of the seven statutory Areas of Experience listed in *Part 2*.

One of the requirements for the teaching of topics is that they should:

> *'be planned and taught in a way which helps pupils develop the knowledge, understanding and skills needed to progress through the levels of attainment in each attainment target'* (page 27).

So we must assume responsibility for all those aspects of classroom management inherent in the Programme of Study.

Getting to know the *Programme of Study Part 1*

- First read pages 23–6 of the ringbinder.
- Then make a list of tasks for the teacher to ensure that pupils have the required opportunities for learning.

Your list might look like this (the numbers refer to the 76 opportunities listed in the ringbinder; the first figure indicates the section and the second figure refers to the statement within that section):

- ensure pupils talk about themselves (1.5, 1.6, etc.)
- organise pairwork and groupwork activities (1.7–1.14, 5.1, etc.)
- provide a range of resources (2.6, 2.12, 4.2, 6.2, etc.)
- find or design a wide range of appropriate activities, including games and improvised drama (3.2, 5.4, 5.5, etc.)
- bring pupils into contact with native speakers here and, if possible, abroad and with adults (4.1, 5.3, etc.)
- keep up to date with own culture and those of the countries and communities where the target language is spoken (4.3, 4.4, 4.6, etc.)
- set up activities outside the classroom (5.2, etc.)
- encourage pupils to work independently (6.1, 6.2, etc.)
- promote the use of computers (6.3, etc.)

In addition, of course, assess while teaching.

So we end up with a job list for the classroom manager! It is not definitive, but it should be useful when we come to look at the teaching strategies we use at present.

Knowing the criteria

Under the heading 'What should I be doing?', it might also be useful to consider what an inspector will be looking for in terms of classroom management. This is no secret. All inspectors are working to a public document. Just as the National Curriculum records what pupils are expected to learn, this document sets out the criteria on which judgements will be made. Different local education authorities have had varying procedures in the past, but with the standardisation of inspection nationally comes a set of national procedures and criteria for judgement. Many aspects of the new inspection system will be familiar to teachers in authorities whose local inspectors have worked to a formalised programme of inspections.

Inspectors will talk to teachers and pupils and will look at teachers' planning and at pupils' work. From lesson observation, they will gather evidence on how teachers create and sustain interest, how they provide for a range of pupil needs and how teaching styles, resources and routines are used to ensure effective learning. Observation is intended to provide departmental evidence on:

- the quality of the teaching
- the quality of the learning, and
- the standards of achievement.

If we link this to our reading of the ringbinder, we can see that pupil learning involves pupil response to the opportunities given to them, while the teaching reflects coverage of the National Curriculum Attainment Targets and the *Programme of Study*. Here lies the challenge in managing the modern languages classroom: to ensure that good quality teaching and good quality learning promote the highest possible standards for all pupils.

Thinking about teaching and learning

- First list all the words and phrases associated with good quality teaching.
- Then list all the words and phrases associated with good quality learning.
- Now compare your lists with those below:

Teaching:	
planning	range of grouping
progression	participation
pace	appropriate methodology
aims	expectations
matching pupils' needs	providing challenge and support
assessment	feedback
motivation	ATs/PoS
range of activities	homework
Learning:	
response to challenge	adaptable
concentration	research skills
commitment	realistic
enjoyment	evaluation
confidence	collaboration
support	success
progress: gains in knowledge, skills and understanding	

What am I doing?

It is very easy to be so busy teaching that you do not have enough time to reflect on how you manage your own classroom. This can make you feel very insecure when someone comes in to watch you teach.

Let's consider three ways of reviewing your practice:

- on your own
- with a colleague
- with the whole department.

Reviewing your practice on your own

- First, list your own strengths and weaknesses to try to come to terms with your teaching style.

For example:

I'm good at:
- getting organised
- motivating pupils
- working with younger pupils
- working with the Assistant
- providing an attractive classroom environment

I'm less good at:
- using the target language with all groups
- setting challenging homework tasks
- afternoon lessons
- following-up on work pupils found difficult
- marking
- keeping the noise level down when pupils are working in groups

- Now look closely at your own list. Some strengths are linked to weaknesses and vice versa. For example: if you are 'good at working with younger pupils', does this mean that your classroom management is less effective with other pupils?

Producing this kind of list may give you an idea of what aspect of classroom management you would like to focus on. On the other hand, it is often more valuable to work with a colleague – and more fun. Why not see if someone could observe you teach and then give you feedback? (*Appraisal for Language Teachers*, another of the handbooks for language teachers in the *Concepts* series, may be useful here – see the booklist on page 29.)

Reviewing with a colleague

- Talk to senior colleagues: make it known that you think having someone in to see you teach is an important part of your staff development and that cover may have to be arranged.
- Give your colleague a particular focus for the observation. For example:
  - ask him or her to produce a list of your strengths and areas for development to compare with your own lists, or
  - ask him or her to work to certain criteria: for example, do you provide for agreed opportunities from the *Programme of Study Part 1* (see the list on page 2)?

Reviewing with the whole department

It can also be useful to work on some aspects of classroom management as a department. This will help to achieve consistency which can be difficult in a large department, in one where the contribution of part-time staff is important or where teachers have whole-school responsibility.

- Choose the particular aspect on which you want to focus: providing opportunities for pupils to develop the ability to work with others, for example.
- Decide on the questions you would want to ask to evaluate your practice. For example: Do we provide pupils with the opportunity to plan and carry out practical and creative activities with a partner or in a group (opportunity 5.1)?
- produce a checklist with two columns for strengths (+) and weaknesses (–), for example:

Programme of Study 1	+	–
5.1 5.2	Yes, with a partner Yes, in class	Not very often in a group Rarely in school and never outside

and so on.

Whether you evaluate your current practice on your own or with a colleague, remember that it is not easy to accept change or to develop new skills, particularly if you have been teaching for a while and feel that the changes are being thrust upon you. So do not expect instant success.

If, for example, you want to move from a limited use of the target language to a more substantial use, this will take time and may be difficult. The graph might look like this:

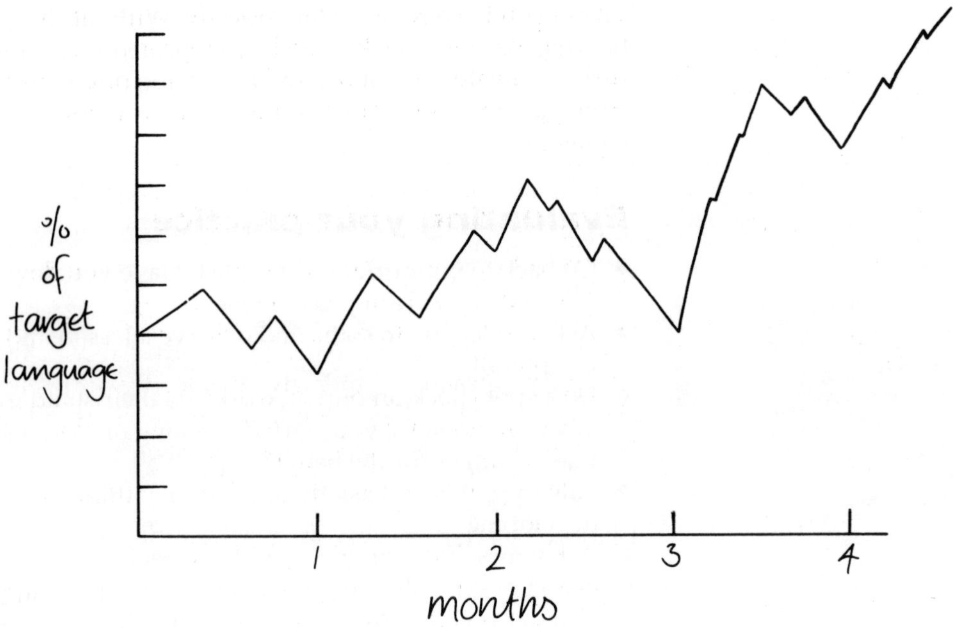

There will be troughs and you may feel despondent. But look at the general direction as your 'management of change' curve evens out and this will make you feel more confident.

What do I want to do next? And how?

Use your audit of current practice to set your goals. But remember not to set goals for the sake of setting them and do not set impossible goals. It is advisable to work on one aspect of your teaching which is not yet in line with National Curriculum requirements, so decide where the priorities are. It can be very rewarding to work on something you have been wanting to improve for a long time.

Setting goals

Ensure your goals are measurable, achievable, specific and timed:

- specific – This is not a general aim, but something very tangible
- measurable – How will you know when you have achieved this goal?
- achievable – Is the goal realistic, given your workload, home life, and so on?
- timed – When must it be achieved by?

For example, your goal might be:

I want to provide more groupwork activities.

Checklist	
Specific	Yes, with my year-10 pupils
Measurable	At least five times a week(?)
Achievable	OK! Three times a week
Timed	For the next month; after that, it will depend how it goes

How will I know if I have been successful?

Good evaluation is an integral part of managing change. A task is not complete unless you have reviewed it critically. Without this process of review, work can become a series of tasks which are repeated but not improved. With pressure on time, the evaluation of our work is all too often missed out. Do not lose this valuable opportunity to recognise what is going well and to identify areas for development.

Evaluating your practice

- Go back to your original checklist. Have you developed any new strengths or reduced any existing weaknesses?
- Ask a colleague to come and observe a lesson and give you feedback (see Chapter 8).
- Do a spot check on pupils' work. Do their standards and presentation reflect any changes since you started working on your classroom management? Are these changes for the better?
- Talk to pupils and ask them what they think and how their learning is developing.
- Ask yourself if you think you have been successful in developing a particular aspect of your classroom management. If so, share this with colleagues, keep it under review and set your next priority.

Hopefully, we can all come to terms with our own strengths and weaknesses. We can then put into action a cycle – **audit, plan, do and review** – which will ensure that our skill in classroom management develops as we build on our growing teaching experience.

Summary

- Identify the overlaps and the gaps between what you're doing and the *Programme of Study Part 1*.
- Make time to consider your own teaching – if possible, with someone else.
- Set your own goals and support them with planning.
- Be pleased with what you achieve and remember that it's a continuous process.

2 You're not on your own!

The role of the teacher has developed and grown. We have always taught both children and our subject; this, in itself, is a dual role. Now we have statutory responsibilities for assessment and recording which mean that we must be consistent in our approach within the department. With these new requirements, many of the classroom management issues may seem new.

You may well find yourself short of time and on your own. Whatever the stage in your career, it is important to welcome discussion with colleagues who can offer support and advice, and who may come to you for the same. Working with colleagues is vital. Sharing experiences is a good way to solve problems and improve practice. It is a useful means of learning informally and, on a more formal level, will promote the openness which is such an important precursor to successful appraisal. Not all colleagues will be used to an open-door policy. However, if someone does want to collaborate or join you in your classroom, welcome this opportunity and ask if you can return the compliment!

The purpose of this chapter is to help you identify the support network available to teachers of languages and to examine collaborative ways of working.

- Who can I work with?
- How do we work together?

Who can I work with?

Think of an occasion when you have asked someone for advice and it has been really useful. In a school, there are many people with a very wide range of specialist skills. Perhaps some of these are colleagues whom you see rarely or irregularly and whose role you may not fully understand. They will not necessarily be linguists and this may make them somewhat apprehensive about working with a foreign language. But they will have their own skills to share and these can enhance our teaching, as long as we make the time to plan together properly.

Identifying your support network

- List all the people, both in school and outside, who may have something to offer to classroom management.
- Develop that list with the help of your colleagues.
- Keep it in your departmental handbook, for reference and updating.

For example:

SEN co-ordinator – Pat Exton (Tel. no. ext. 31)	Experience in assessment, personalised work programmes, differentiation, work with the more able.

Repromaster A (page 30) provides a format for recording your ideas. Use the column entitled 'Details' to keep a note of useful information with each colleague. Repromaster B (page 31) provides an example of a handout which might stimulate discussion on the range of colleagues available. Remember, though, that these are only suggestions and it should be your own notes which go into your departmental handbook.

How do we work together?

Have you ever been told something really important in the corridor? It is a common enough way of exchanging news in a school. However, if you are seeking to improve your classroom management by collaborating with a colleague, it is much better to arrange a meeting and discuss the matter carefully in advance.

Where there will be two teachers in the classroom, detailed planning for the lesson is vital. It can be very demotivating for a Special Educational Needs (SEN) teacher or a foreign language assistant to sit in a foreign language lesson and feel useless. Colleagues working together need to understand each other's needs and skills.

Time spent at the beginning of a joint venture is time well invested. It will make future planning much easier and more effective. Classroom management, too, will be significantly enhanced if pupils see a purposeful relationship between two teachers. Both must be equal partners and have equal status in the eyes of the pupils.

Planning your collaboration

- Ensure that your head of department knows of your intended collaboration.
- Discuss the following questions with your colleague:
  - What is the purpose of the collaboration?
  - What is the role of each teacher?
  - What time commitment can each of us make?
  - What preparation do we both need to do?
  - What do we hope to gain from the collaboration?
  - What do we hope the pupils will gain?
  - How will we know if our collaboration has been successful?
- If you will be working together in the classroom, also consider the following:
  - What are the objectives of the lesson?
  - What is the particular focus for each teacher – for example, a particular group of pupils or a particular activity?
  - What do we both consider to be an acceptable noise level?
  - What are the respective roles with regard to managing pupils' behaviour?
  - Will pupils be allowed free movement around the classroom?
- Show your colleague the teaching area, its resources and equipment.

If you are lucky enough to have another adult in your lesson, it is important to ensure that your style of classroom management is supportive of their role. Any form of independent learning (resource-based learning, pairwork or groupwork) lends itself particularly well to paired teaching.

Identifying your roles

- Consider the suitability of these roles for two teachers working together in the classroom:
  - Both do a joint presentation – for example, a role play – and then circulate.
  - One leads, the other circulates supporting pupils.
  - One leads, the other works with an individual or a particular group of pupils.
  - One leads, the other withdraws a particular group for an agreed activity.
  - One teaches, the other carries out assessment.
  - One teaches, the other observes (see Chapter 8).
  - One leads, pupils undertake a series of activities and the other monitors learning on one activity – for example, computer work.
- When your ongoing discussion of needs and skills is well under way, begin your planning, taking into account the importance of clearly understood roles for both teachers.
- After the lesson, make time to review how things went. This will ensure that the collaboration is given the best chance of success.

Evaluating your work

- Consider these questions:
  - Which aspects of the lesson went particularly well?
  - Did you both feel useful throughout?
  - Did pupils understand why they had two teachers?
  - Is there anything you would improve for next time?

Many teachers feel a little uneasy about having another adult in their classroom, particularly if they are not used to this. It is a sensitive issue and good communication and trust between both teachers are vital. Good communication, after all, is what it is all about.

Summary

- Identify and make contact with other people with whom you can work.
- If you are going to work as a pair or in a team, plan your work together and allocate your roles carefully.

3 Your classroom and you

The purpose of this chapter is to identify ways in which the provision of a stimulating learning environment can set a positive tone for language learning.

- What is my classroom like?
- How can I make the best use of my classroom?
- How can I use the learning environment in my lessons?

What is my classroom like?

Your classroom creates an atmosphere which speaks volumes about you and what you have to offer your pupils. A well-kept and attractive classroom with relevant displays will promote more responsible behaviour from pupils, especially if their contributions to the appearance of the classroom are valued by you and by their own friends. For the busy teacher, the layout and appearance of the classroom can slip down the list of priorities. However, there is no doubt that any time invested in developing your learning environment will be of benefit both to you and to your pupils. Your classroom will become a better place in which to teach and learn!

Improving the learning environment

- Draw up a list of statements, on your own or with colleagues, which describe a stimulating languages classroom.
- Tick every statement which describes your classroom.
- Put a question mark next to any statement if you need to confer with someone before making any improvement.
- Put an exclamation mark if the improvement is easy to make.
- Put an arrow if the improvement requires longer-term planning.
- Then make a list identifying your own short- and long-term priorities.

For example:

• The door of the classroom is welcoming (e.g. poster with *Bienvenue*, *Hier spricht man deutsch* or *Aquí se habla español*)	√
• The layout of the tables looks tidy	√
• The room is free of litter	!
• The teacher's desk is tidy	!
• There are no items (e.g. a torn blind) requiring maintenance	?
• Storage facilities are adequate and easy to keep tidy	?
• Materials for pupils (e.g. dictionaries, readers) are clearly labelled	!
• All electrical equipment is safely positioned	?
• The board is clean or ready for the next lesson	!
• The display boards are neatly backed and mounted	←
• The posters are relevant to current classwork	←
• Pupils' work is on display	√
• Pupils have been involved in mounting the display	←
• Display is used in lessons	←
• There are personal touches in the room (e.g. plants, photos)	√
• The room is carpeted and has black-out facilities	?

My short-term priorities are:
1 Include checking room for litter and cleaning board as part of the clearing away procedure at the end of each lesson. Write in lesson plan book as a reminder!
2 Tidy teacher's desk.
3 Label shelves. Maybe ask pupils to prepare labels on computer?
4 Arrange for torn blind and faulty window to be repaired.
5 Arrange maintenance check for electrical equipment.
6 Discuss storage facilities, carpets and black-outs with head of department.

My longer-term priorities are:
1 Sort out display boards (back of room by half-term, side walls by end of term).
2 Check all available posters and decide where they best fit into scheme of work.
3 Discuss with colleagues how to make best use of display in lessons. Maybe share ideas at a departmental meeting?
4 Identify a few pupils in each class who might like to have responsibility for part of the classroom display – have a meeting with all of them after half-term to plan.

Your response to these questions will probably vary according to the stage in the year or the term, or according to which group of pupils last used your room. There may be some questions which you decide not to address. Whatever your response, improving the learning environment should be seen as part of a continual process. The crucial thing is to identify where you are going next!

'But I don't have my own classroom!'

The teacher without a permanent base faces particular difficulties, having to adapt and respond to different situations. Some improvements can be made by discussion with other colleagues who use the room. Obviously, when planning the lesson, you need to take into account the classroom where you teach. However, if classroom management difficulties arise from working away from a base or if some of the opportunities specified in *Programme of Study Part 1* cannot be offered to pupils in a non-languages classroom, this is a matter for concern and should be discussed with the head of department as soon as possible. It should be possible to re-arrange classes in such a way that each group of pupils has at least one lesson a week in a languages room, with access to displays, the overhead projector, dictionaries, etc. Perhaps the majority of the active work could take place in the languages classroom with a particular focus on using the video- and tape-recorder in the non-languages classroom (if they are easily accessible).

Whatever you decide, individual planning and planning at departmental level are inextricably linked and should be a high priority in this situation.

How can I make the best use of my classroom?

The best starting point is to have a tidy classroom. Pupils entering the room will sense a 'ready-for-work' atmosphere. This part of the chapter will consider three key aspects in more detail:

- layout of tables
- use of equipment and resources
- displays.

Classroom layout often determines the success of activities

The requirements for a languages classroom will probably be different to those for other areas of the curriculum. Pupils must be able to see and hear the teacher when new vocabulary is presented, move easily into pairwork, hear the cassette, see the OHP or video, work independently, work in groups, play language games, take part in improvised drama and use a wide range of resources.

Your choice of classroom layout is a variable depending on the size of your room, the classes you teach, your own style of teaching and the particular activity. However, the following points might be worth considering:

- A double horseshoe arrangement enables the majority of pupils to see one another. This is vital if pupils are to be able to hear one another in oral work.
- The teacher is often the focal point of the classroom during the presentation stage, but it may not be necessary for the teacher's desk to be a focal point. Space can be saved by moving the desk slightly to one side. You can then discuss work with individual pupils at your desk whilst keeping an eye on the rest of the class.
- There must be sufficient space between the desks (and this will affect your choice of layout) for you to move around the class, especially when monitoring oral work. You will need to be quite close to pupils to hear them if the whole class is practising a speaking task. Your classroom layout must also be practical so that pupils can get out quickly in the rare event of an emergency.
- A change of seating arrangement often creates interest. There may be occasions when you can move all the desks to the side and create a large space in the centre of the room. Pupils could sit on chairs in a circle (with a notebook, if necessary) for extended speaking practice, games or drama. Similarly, if you are planning extended language work using the OHP or video, it might be worth getting pupils to arrange their chairs in semi-circles near the equipment.
- If you have a regular layout of tables for most activities, it might be worth encouraging pupils to sit in particular places. This may help to break the often rigid boy/girl divide in many classrooms.
- A tape-recorder operated from the centre area of the room or from a raised position will be easier to hear than one operated from the front desk. Wall-mounted speakers are quite cheap and have significant advantages.

Choosing your classroom layout

- Draw sketches of the table arrangements possible in your classroom.
- Discuss the possibilities with a colleague in the department and identify which layout is most appropriate for each type of activity in the languages classroom.
- Consider the position of the teacher's desk, equipment and resources in each case.

Using equipment and resources should be easy for everyone

Gone are the days when the teacher alone operated any equipment or distributed any resources in the room! Pupils should now feel that using the computer, making a presentation using the OHP, operating the tape-recorder, video and video camera and referring to a variety of resources are all part of the normal activities in a languages classroom.

Using equipment and resources

Carry out an audit of current practice using the range of symbols on page 10. Then identify your priorities. For example:

- The department shares all its equipment and resources [?]
- All classes have equal access to equipment and resources [!]
- Resources for pupils to use are easily accessible and clearly labelled [!]
- Pupils are given regular opportunities to use a variety of equipment and resources [?]
- Boys and girls are using the equipment equally [!]
- Health and safety aspects of the equipment are reviewed regularly [!]
- The storage procedure is easy to use [←]
- Out-of-date materials are thrown away [?]

Priorities for next term:

1 Suggest that the department establishes a rota for video and computer.
2 Use the computer equally with all groups.
3 Try (again!) to get lockers replaced by shelving.
4 Book safety check for equipment.
5 Suggest that reading materials are organised into different levels.

You could run through these statements regularly and identify the next priority. As part of a departmental process, it might be a particularly useful activity at the end or start of a term. Teachers will be at different stages along the way to managing a multi-purpose classroom. It doesn't matter where you are, but it is worth spending time reviewing how you currently use the equipment and resources in your room. It is essential to have a clear idea of your next priority for improving the quality of access to equipment and resources for your pupils.

The display in your classroom brings your lessons alive

The majority of language classrooms are used as tutor rooms and many are used by other teachers during the course of a week. It is worth spending time with all colleagues who use the room to identify everybody's needs and plan accordingly.

Secondary teachers can learn much from primary colleagues about display and it is worth a visit to a feeder school to look specifically at display. If you offer a taster lesson to pupils who are about to transfer from primary school, why not encourage those pupils to contribute to a display as one of the possible outcomes? This could then be on display in the languages area or classrooms at the start of the new year so that the new pupils will feel particularly welcome.

The start of the year is usually a good time to start from scratch with your classroom display. Obviously, there will need to be a space for all the business information (e.g. fire notice, tutor group notices), but there are many ways of grouping other displays. Each year group could have an allocated space or there could be a thematic display (e.g. on food) including work from a variety of year groups. It is important to have a balance of languages on display – it can be disconcerting for a pupil learning German or Spanish or Italian to be surrounded by French-only displays! If you have target language phrases on display, it would be a good idea to colour-code the phrases to avoid any confusion for pupils.

Making the most of displays

- Consider your display under the following headings:
  Permanent reference – this could include reference materials, such as the spelling of numbers, case tables or support for the use of target language e.g. posters or vocabulary mobiles (see page 14).
  Temporary reference – this could include current areas of vocabulary or support for a grammatical point e.g. past participles.

Evidence of pupils' achievement – this should include contributions from all classes you teach and, during the course of a year, try to include something from every pupil. It might be worth identifying two or three artistically-minded pupils in each class to be responsible for mounting the display and keeping it looking tidy. Suggestions for interesting opportunities for work leading to a display could be incorporated into the scheme of work.

Equality of opportunity – this could include consideration of gender, disability, age and ethnic origin. For example, are the activities depicted shared equally between men and women? Do the displays reflect ethnic diversity, feature a range of ages, include people who are disabled?

Cultural context – this could be in the form of posters, photographs, realia, leaflets, etc., and should present as broad a picture of the countries of the languages studied as possible. If you have a foreign language assistant, a small area of display could be mounted and changed regularly by the assistant, focusing on his or her family, home, town, interests, etc.

- Identify a few targets for possible improvement during the next term. For example:
  1. Have one column in the register/mark book headed 'Display' and tick whenever a pupil's work contributes to the classroom display.
  2. Talk to the foreign language assistant about possible contributions to the display area.

How can I use the learning environment in my lessons?

If all the display in your classroom is relevant to the current activities or to the pupils you teach, it should be easy to integrate it into lessons. For example:

- **The display can provide the activity:**
  - Pupils can write letters describing their homes. The letters are then displayed. You, the foreign language assistant or a pupil work out quiz questions for the pupils to answer by reading the letters.
- **The display can provide reference for an activity:**
  - A poster with past participles will be useful for pupils working on an information-gap speaking activity based on last week's diary.
  - Vocabulary support can be provided on posters or mobiles. For example:

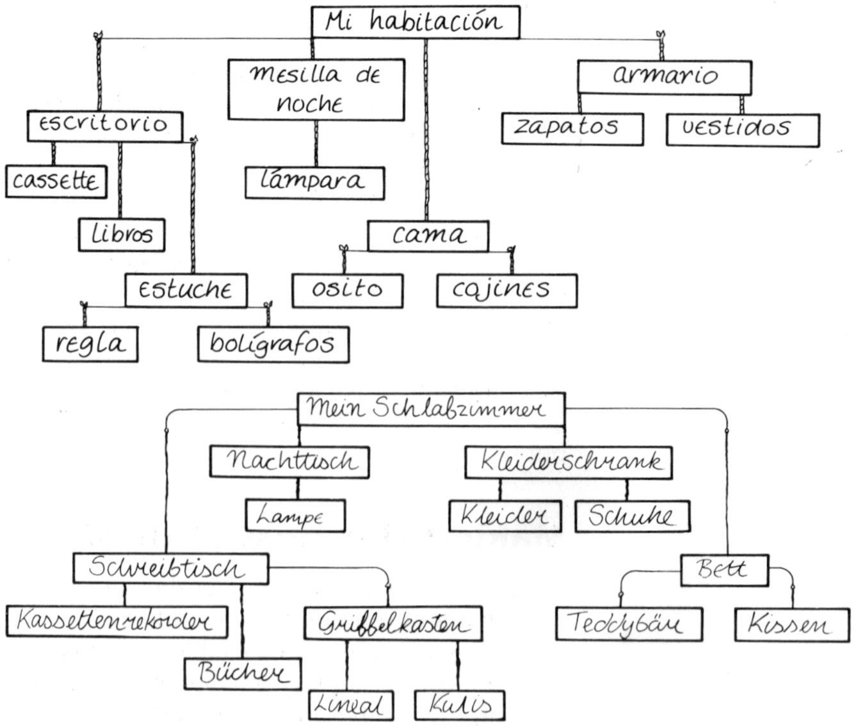

Mobiles for vocabulary support

- **The display can provide extension activities:**
  - Pupils use a series of pictures or photos on display as a stimulus for writing poems, either on their own or in groups.
- **The display can provide a summary of an activity:**
  - The front page of a newspaper can be designed by pupils to describe a crime or an accident.
  - The results of a class survey on hobbies can be put on display (graphs, pie charts, diagrams, etc.).

The profile of languages in the school is considerably enhanced by extending good quality display into the corridors and around the school. Labelling rooms and putting up notices such as *¡Bienvenido a nuestro instituto! Keine Schultaschen in der Kantine, bitte! Pas de chewing gum!* in all the languages spoken by pupils in the school offer a valuable opportunity for promoting languages. Also, cross-curricular displays provide an added dimension to work in languages. For example, if the science department has a display on healthy eating, the languages department can add to this display with graphs from class surveys, posters promoting healthy lifestyles, and so on. These might arise from your work in class and might contribute to a display in another part of the school.

Summary

- Think critically about the effectiveness of your classroom as a learning environment.
- Plan to make the most of layout, display, equipment and resources inside and outside the classroom.
- Use your classroom as a resource, not just a teaching space.

4 Lesson planning for the National Curriculum

The purpose of this chapter is to offer detailed guidance on planning lessons for the National Curriculum.

- Where do I start?
- How do I plan?

Where do I start?

Whether you are newly qualified or a very experienced teacher, it is important to review your lesson-planning process regularly. Your lesson plan is the formal record of what you plan on a day-to-day basis. There are several features of a lesson plan which are directly related to classroom management issues. Some of these may be instinctive to you; all of them will benefit from reconsideration as the National Curriculum comes on stream.

In the light of the requirements of the National Curriculum, many departments are reviewing the way in which they plan lessons. Not only do pupils have to be offered certain statutory opportunities (see the *Programme of Study Part 1*) but ongoing assessment is now an integral part of the teaching and learning process. These National Curriculum requirements should be evident in the lesson plan. The main starting point, then, for any lesson plan should be the departmental scheme of work which will be related to the National Curriculum.

How do I plan?

If classroom management is about managing pupils' learning, then the lesson plan is a crucial part of our preparation. The important part of lesson planning is the thinking time, not the writing down. In addition to pacing your lesson appropriately, it is important to pace yourself. It would be unrealistic to expect every lesson to be planned in minute detail. You might plan most lessons in broad terms with certain lessons planned in detail. However, it is important to have clear targets for yourself as part of the developmental process of improving your classroom management skills and to ensure that each group receives an equal share of your detailed planning. If a department is focusing on improving the quality of the learning experience, then the following activity could form a useful part of a departmental workshop.

Deciding what's in a lesson plan

- Write a list of all the aspects which will affect the way you plan your lesson. For example:

– the learning objectives and how to communicate these to pupils
– the length of the lesson (single or double)
– the time of the lesson (morning or afternoon, after PE/drama?)
– your energy levels
– the group of pupils
– the pace of lesson appropriate to the group
– the ability range within the group (extension/support activities)
– the classroom environment (languages or non-languages room)
– the stage reached in the topic

- the variety of activities and the amount of pupil movement involved
- assessment opportunities
- the equipment and resources available
- whether you are on your own or with another colleague, such as FLA, SEN support teacher (see Chapter 2)
- maximum use of target language
- basic routines (taking register, setting homework)
- the balance of skills
- progression

- Identify the implications for classroom management.
  Your classroom management must be such that:
  - you provide pupils with the opportunity to achieve the lesson objectives
  - you have ways of recording that performance
  - you leave yourself time to record how they did and plan for future lessons accordingly.

  This way of planning means that assessment is an integral part of classroom management.
- Consider a recent lesson plan in the light of the aspects you have identified:
  - Which aspects did you take into account?
  - Which aspects might you need to consider in more detail next time?
- Identify one realistic target for yourself. It is unrealistic to take on too much at a time. For example, you might identify a lack of assessment opportunities. Plan to include one activity from which you will record pupil performance against the National Curriculum levels.
- Design a proforma, either on your own or with colleagues, which will help you plan your lessons effectively. You might like to consider the example on repromaster C (page 32) as a starting point. However, this type of proforma is obviously very detailed and could therefore only be used for some lessons. It would be unrealistic to expect to be able to fill in that amount of detail for all lessons. A completed version of the lesson plan is given on repromaster D (page 33).

Each lesson needs to have a pattern: the importance of routines should not be underestimated. A shared sense of security is particularly important in speaking activities, if pupils are to learn without inhibition. No matter how good the teaching activity, effective differentiation can only occur if pupils feel at ease in the lesson. Pupils feel secure in a classroom where the routines and ground rules for behaviour are clear (see Chapter 5). It is important that these routines are consistent across the department to avoid unnecessary difficulties when pupils have a change of teacher. If routines are well-established and planning is good, pupils' behaviour should also be good. Similarly, high pupil expectations should be encouraged – for example, pupils are more likely to arrive on time and settle quickly for a lesson which starts promptly and efficiently.

Identifying routines and activities

- Identify routines and activities that happen nearly every lesson.
- Decide how you are going to approach each routine and activity.

This could be done individually or, better still, as a department.

The following example may be a useful starting point:

Taking the register: At the start of a lesson, each pupil responds in the target language (for example, telling you an interesting fact about themselves or one activity they did last weekend or giving you an item of vocabulary relevant to the current topic).

Establishing silence: Call out *'Silence, s'il vous plaît'* and count down from five. By the time you get to zero, the class should be silent. A good technique is to get the class to join in the countdown, because any pupils who did not hear your original instruction to be quiet will soon realise what is happening. A non-verbal strategy is to raise your arm as a signal for silence and the pupils follow suit, becoming silent as they do so!

Changing activities: The *'Silence'* techniques could be used to bring the class to order. Pupils will find it supportive to hear the same phrase used to signal a change of activity, for example: *'On change'*. These phrases should form part of the departmental list of target language phrases.
Setting homework: Set homework in the target language, but also write homework on the board, in English if necessary. For example: Say *'Hausaufgaben für nächsten Montag. Schreibt die Details ins Heft* (accompanied by mime). *Lest den Artikel auf Seite 24. Sind die Sätze unten richtig oder falsch? Schreibt die Antworten ins Heft.'* Write on board: *H/W – Monday. Read article – page 24. True or false answers in book*. As pupils become more confident, a pupil could listen to the instructions and write the details on the board.
Start of lesson: Five minutes of quick question-and-answer work or revision of vocabulary. This can be useful to set a positive atmosphere and provide continuity from the previous foreign language lesson.
Collecting books: Stand by the door and collect books as pupils leave. This gives an opportunity for social niceties, such as: *'Merci/Au revoir/Tu as bien travaillé aujourd'hui!'*
Returning books: If possible, books should be on the desk as pupils arrive. One or two pupils could return books quietly as the class comes in.

Patterns and routines must remain flexible. You may decide to change plans depending on the circumstances. For example, you may have planned a very active lesson without realising that the lesson would be interrupted every few minutes for pupils to have their BCG injections! Or pupils may be totally engrossed in a collaborative writing task and it would be inappropriate to stop the groups to embark on a listening activity for the last ten minutes.

One of the best ways of reviewing a lesson plan prior to teaching it is to consider these two questions:
- What will I be doing?
- What will individual pupils be doing?

Summary

- Give yourself time to plan properly.
- Review your usual planning and refine it as necessary around a clear structure of routines.

5 Designing activities

The purpose of this chapter is to consider some of the key features of successful learning activities.

- How do I design a series of learning activities?

How do I design a series of learning activities?

Your lesson plan will refer both to chosen activities from course materials and to activities which you have designed yourself. Successful classroom management depends on your choice of challenging but realistic activities. Designing successful learning activities, therefore, is closely linked to effective classroom management. The better the activity, the more manageable your lesson. It doesn't matter whether the pupils are doing the activity on their own, in pairs or in groups: the principles for activity design are the same. They require careful development of the language skills and content to ensure progression in pupil learning.

Developing a set of basic visuals for each topic sets a firm foundation for sustaining the use of the target language.

Introducing the activity

- Identify the *key vocabulary* for a topic and develop visuals or cues. For example, making a date (in French):

Days of week	Times	Activities	Meeting places
	19:45 10:00 12:15 18:45		

- Identify the *key phrases* for a topic and develop visuals or cues. For example:

Tu es libre samedi matin?	Samedi matin?
Tu veux aller au cinéma?	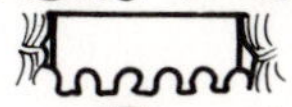 ?
On se rencontre à quelle heure?	 ?
Où est-ce qu'on se retrouve?	Rendez-vous?

- Lead in to the presentation of a model dialogue, using the OHP (if you have one) or flashcards, perhaps with the foreign language assistant, and then some teacher–pupil practice. Thorough preparation ensures clear understanding of the task and best possible accents!

Designing the practice activities

- Decide which of the following kinds of activity best suit your pupils' current needs. They are all in line with National Curriculum requirements for pupil opportunities:

1 Repetitive; good for reinforcement (see PoS 1.7, AT2, 1a, etc.).
2 Closed; good for basic practice (see PoS 1.8, AT2, 2b, etc.).
3 Information-gap; often motivating (see PoS 1.2, AT2, 3a, etc.).
4 Open-ended; useful towards the end of a topic for consolidation (see PoS 1.10, AT1, 7a, etc.).
5 Unpredictable; keeps pupils on their toes (see PoS 1.9, 1.11, 1.12, 1.14, AT2, 6a, etc.).
6 Carousel; sets a firm pace, but can be frustrating for pupils if they have to change activity before fully completing the previous one.
7 Drama preparation; motivates well, but how do you ensure that all pupils contribute fully (see PoS 5.5, etc.)?
8 Problem-solving; challenging for pupils, but how do you ensure that all pupils are involved (see PoS 1.9, AT2, 7a, etc.)?
9 Assignment; relies on pupils to take the initiative (see PoS 5.6, etc.).

These are not discrete categories and many activities will have a mixture of features. For example, a survey may use several closed questions as well as one or two with unpredictable answers; a carousel may include closed tasks or provide preparation for an assignment.

Examples of all these activities are given on repromasters E and F at the back of the book (pages 34–5).

- Identify the features of good practice for activity design, for example:
  - clear instructions
  - variety of tasks
  - variety of media
  - use of target language
  - use of support materials
  - time limit
  - self-marking
  - end product.
- Decide which features are appropriate for your activity.
- Discuss the production of materials and storage. It might be worth trialling materials and reviewing them at the end of the year. With departmental agreement you can then produce good quality materials, perhaps laminated on card, and a filing system which will mean that the following year should be easier.

Chapter 7 provides guidance on strategies for recording pupil progress. If you are to be able to manage your recording effectively, your planning must indicate:

- which activities are appropriate for recording
- which SoAs the activities reflect/cover
- when you will record pupils' achievements
- what form your recording will take.

Summary

- Plan a series of activities which have:
  - visuals
  - variety
  - opportunities for consolidation
  - opportunities for extension
  - opportunities for recording.

6 Working with pupils in groups

Part 1 of the *Programme of Study* describes the opportunities teachers must provide to enable pupils to develop their language skills. All of these opportunities must be offered in the target language. The sections entitled *'Developing the ability to work with others'* and *'Developing the ability to learn independently'* are closely related. Pupils who work independently know how to help themselves. This makes them potentially valuable group members. Successful pairwork and groupwork depend on a style of classroom management which ensures that all pupils:

- understand what they are doing
- have individual access to stimulus and reference materials
- have strategies for asking for help in the target language
- work in an orderly learning environment.

Pupils need to know what is expected of them and an agreed set of ground rules will form a basis for good pupil–teacher understanding and can be displayed in your classroom.

The purpose of this chapter is to examine some of the principles underlying effective pairwork and groupwork.

- What are the ground rules for pupils?
- How do I group pupils?
- How do I manage the groups?

What are the ground rules for pupils?

Ground rules must be agreed collaboratively and reinforced constantly. They are rules designed to facilitate learning.

Setting ground rules

- Decide what the ground rules for your classroom might be. For example:

> We speak Spanish here.
> We talk quietly.
> We don't eat chewing gum in class.
> We write down our homework.
> We help each other.
> We don't distract other people in the lesson.
> We are all equal in this classroom.

- Compare these rules with those of your colleagues.
- Ask pupils if there are any others they think are important.
- Agree a departmental set of ground rules for foreign language learning.
- Translate them into the target language(s) so that they can be used as a prioritising activity for pupils.
- Ask the pupils, in groups, to select the five they think are most important for their group.
- Collate responses to identify the top five ground rules for the class.
- Display the rules in your classroom.

By giving pupils the opportunity to identify their own priorities, you will hopefully have made an important step towards establishing a good atmosphere for learning.

How do I group pupils?

The relationships between pupils produce a dynamic which can make or break lessons. It is important that the nature of the activity should determine how pupils are grouped. Appropriate grouping will enhance learning, whether pupils are working in pairs or groups of six.

Choosing groupings

- Consider the following types of group. Are there any you might wish to add?
  - Friendship
  - Mixed-ability
  - Ability
  - Mixed-gender
  - Single-gender
  - Random
  - Interest
- Identify which groupings might be most appropriate for the following types of activity:
  - Groupwork assignments
  - Surveys
  - Speaking tasks at the beginning of a new topic
  - Games
  - Creative and imaginative work
  - Consolidation and extension activities
  - Working on the computer.
- Discuss the appropriateness of the different ways of grouping. Repromaster G on page 36 may be useful to record your discussion.

The groups are there to promote learning, so be firm and don't let the forming of groups cause delay. If you have already decided on the groups, stop pupils at the door and direct them accordingly. If you want random groupings, here are some ideas:

Counting off: In a class of 30, if you want groups of three, number each pupil from one to ten, then ask all those who are number one to join together, and so on.

Birthdays: Ask pupils to group together according to the month of their birthday. (This will not give you even-sized groups.)

Topic groups: Distribute cue cards relating to a topic. Ask pupils to find the rest of their group. For example:

Pupil A: **Qu'est-ce que tu fais ce soir?**
Pupil B: *(holding card and showing cinema symbol)*
Je voudrais aller au cinéma.
Pupil A: *(also holding card and showing cinema symbol)*
Moi aussi.

Valuable feedback on the effects of pupil grouping can be gained from an observer: would a colleague be happy to help?

How do I manage the groups?

Get involved by circulating to check that all pupils are doing their task. Monitor at least one group's work in detail.

Recording: decide in advance what to record (see Chapter 7).

Only interrupt groupwork when you have listened to what pupils are saying and watched them carefully.

Untidy written work (for example, notes from listening activity) means that you need to think carefully about the activity and the method of recording it.

Pace the lesson firmly, but in response to pupil needs. This is both important and difficult. Feedback from an observer or pupils can be useful.

Set aside time to clear up.

Summary

- Establish an understanding with pupils of the importance of positive attitudes to learning: agree ground rules.
- If you want pupils to work together, organise groups which are appropriate for the activity and for the pupils.
- Be clear about your role when pupils are working in groups – preparation and organisation must be complemented by sensitive support and careful monitoring.

7 The importance of recording

The purpose of this chapter is to consider some of the ways in which careful recording is an essential part of classroom management.

- Why are records important?
- What should I record? And how?

Why are records important?

Teachers have a statutory responsibility to keep National Curriculum records which must be available to parents, colleagues and governors. However, you will also want to keep records to document what goes on in your classroom, to assess the progress of your pupils and to plan future work. Record-keeping has always been part of a teacher's work, but the extent to which the traditional mark book has been helpful in describing the progress of an individual pupil or useful in informing future practice is now being questioned. Record-keeping is only effective if it really does provide an accurate picture of the development of pupil learning. Assessment provides vital evidence on the standards your pupils are achieving. For example, how does the achievement of the boys compare with that of the girls?

This chapter offers some ideas on recording. Be realistic and set yourself one target at a time!

What should I record? And how?

The departmental scheme of work provides the broad programme for a group of pupils, but lesson plans, especially those which have been annotated and evaluated after the actual lesson (see Chapter 4), will provide a detailed record of the activities which took place in your classroom. In terms of the National Curriculum, it is important to ensure that pupils are being offered the 76 opportunities outlined in the *Programme of Study Part 1*. Cross-referencing occasional lessons or a series of lessons with those 76 opportunities will help you become more familiar with them and, as a result, the process will become quicker. You will soon get to know that opportunity 1.11 is 'take part in structured and less structured role-play'. You will also get to know that few lessons provide for opportunity 1.15: 'adjust language to suit context, audience and purpose'. But it can be refreshing to realise just how many opportunities pupils are being offered each lesson!

Recording opportunities

- Conduct an audit of a recent lesson, by cross-referencing each activity with the opportunities specified in the *Programme of Study Part 1*.
- Read through the opportunities which were not offered during the lesson.
- Identify those opportunities which could easily be incorporated into future lessons and plan how to incorporate the less easy ones over the next few terms.

An example of a lesson plan which has been cross-referenced with the opportunities has been provided on repromaster D (page 33).

We can use the *Programme of Study Part 1* to plan the range of activities in our lessons and the statements of attainment (SoAs) for assessment. This means that we need to know those statements really well to incorporate appropriate activities into our planning. The process of getting to know the statements will highlight the implications for classroom management.

Getting to know the statements of attainment

- Choose any statement of attainment (SoA). For example:
  AT1, 4b: 'identify and note specific and significant details in longer familiar messages or dialogues'.
- Identify the implications for your classroom management.
  You need to:
  - provide pupils with opportunities to do this
  - have ways of recording that performance
  - plan for future lessons according to their performance.

Whichever statement you choose, the implications will be the same. We need to be skilled in designing activities which allow pupils to show progress through the statements of attainment. We also need to have realistic means of recording this. Nobody is saying this is not a mammoth task! Talk to colleagues at Key Stages 1 and 2 or in other curriculum areas where they have been through this process. Instead of marking end of unit tests, we must now spend time considering how best to integrate assessment into everyday classroom management. This is certainly a professional challenge but the process should be more rewarding for pupils and teachers than those endless piles of marking.

Your department needs to have a system for recording National Curriculum information for individual pupils. The simpler the proforma, the better! Ideally, you should be able to fill it in as you circulate, watching pupils work. Alternatively, identify lessons when you have a few minutes after the lesson to fill in the information. The proforma should give an 'at a glance' picture of the progress of a pupil. Examples of proformas are given on repromasters H and I (pages 37–8) but it would be wise for each department to develop its own proforma to meet its own requirements.

In addition, evidence of pupils' achievement should be kept to complement the information on the proforma. *'It* (collecting evidence) *should be seen as part of teachers' everyday work and not an additional task required by the National Curriculum'* (SEAC, 1992). Again, we need to develop an effective and manageable way of achieving this.

A good way of keeping evidence is to develop a portfolio of work for each pupil. Pupils themselves may be familiar with the idea from their primary schools and records of achievement. Pupils may be able to decide which pieces of work they would like to keep as evidence of their achievement and their involvement in this process should be encouraged. Any work kept in the portfolio must be annotated to provide the context and the level of attainment.

Collecting evidence

- Select a variety of pieces of pupils' work across the four attainment targets. This will be much easier for AT4 (writing), so careful planning is needed to provide evidence for the other three skills.
- Consider the range of information that might be useful under 'Context' to make the annotated work a useful piece of evidence (e.g. stimulus/source, with/without help/reference materials, alone/in pairs/groups, homework?).
- Discuss the implications of storage, including cassettes and copies of written work.
- Annotate the pieces of work using a sticker such as this one:

Name:	**Tutor group:**	
Date:	**AT:**	**Level:**
Context:		

An example of a piece of work annotated in this way is given on repromaster J (page 39). This evidence can then be stored in the pupil's portfolio folder. It is important to remember that work stored should demonstrate recent achievement. A pupil who is consistently working at levels 4 and 5 does not need to keep evidence of work at levels 1–3. Information about the pupil's progress through those earlier levels will have been documented on a proforma such as the one on repromaster I (page 38).

It should be stressed that agreeing the types of work that demonstrate performance at a particular level is an essential activity for the department. Even so, interpreting the levels on your own is not always easy. A moderating meeting with colleagues to compile a departmental portfolio with examples of pupils' work across the attainment targets and the levels provides a useful reference point for the whole department.

Many teachers express concern about how to assess progress in speaking. Obviously, pupils could record certain speaking activities onto a cassette as part of their portfolio of evidence. This could be an outcome from working with the assistant or a paired activity. If you want pupils to record their work, you will need to bear this in mind when you are doing your planning to ensure that the equipment and suitable conditions are available.

Your own judgement of a pupil's performance in speaking will be vital, but it will be important to note the context of any work. Teacher notes or a teacher diary are possible ways of recording this vital information. Develop the habit of jotting things down in a notebook or on your lesson plan. This may mean that you have to become selective in what you mark. If your lesson plan identifies an activity as an ideal opportunity to assess speaking and the context is noted in the lesson plan, it may well be sufficient to note the date and level for each pupil heard, as more precise details could be checked back in the lesson plan. A teacher diary, a kind of 'jotter', is also useful to make brief notes about the date and context of a speaking task performed successfully by certain pupils. An example of a teacher diary is given on repromaster K (page 40).

Finally, there is a very easy way of recording progress – praise your pupils! It is important to recognise the value of praising pupils' achievement. Pupils of all abilities need to feel that their work is valued and that their progress is being monitored and recorded. A positive teacher who offers praise where it is due will encourage pupils to learn, and motivating pupils is, after all, the key to successful classroom management.

Summary

- Understand your statutory responsibility to record pupils' progress.
- Get to know the statements of attainment, collect evidence, agree a departmental approach and leave yourself enough time for recording.

8 Taking your practice forward

The purpose of this chapter is to promote regular review of classroom management procedures by offering ideas for mutual observation between colleagues.

- Where do I go from here?

Where do I go from here?

In Chapter 1 we said that the cycle '**audit, plan, do and review**' is vital to ensure that classroom management develops by building on growing teaching experience. It is important to follow through each stage of the cycle; short circuiting will make the whole process less effective.

All teachers will probably have been observed and some of these experiences will have been positive, some less so. Classroom observation can be a very useful means of reviewing practice, highlighting and developing strengths and supporting change. It depends on trust, on the observer being seen as a partner, not an intruder. (See *Appraisal for Language Teachers* in ALL/MGP *Concepts* series.)

Have a meeting beforehand with the colleague you are going to work with to agree on practical details and on the important aspects of what you will be doing. What will you say to pupils who want to know why there is another teacher in the classroom, writing notes? Are there enough chairs and where will your observer sit? You will both need to agree the criteria to which the observation notes will be written and a format for those notes.

There will probably be examples of lesson observation schedules in your school or you may prefer to develop your own. Keep the format simple and factual: write down what happens rather than your opinions. Keep a note of any questions you want to ask. It can also be useful to keep a note of timings.

Planning the observation

- Identify a colleague or colleagues to work with.
- Discuss your experiences of being observed (in case the air needs clearing!) and agree the best way to proceed.
- Agree what good classroom management involves. You might find it useful to refer back to the list drawn up in Chapter 1 – 'Thinking about teaching and learning' – on page 3! This will give you a set of criteria for the observation.
- Discuss your expectations of each other. For example: Will the observer circulate? Will he or she stay for the whole lesson?
- Decide how you will record the observation.
- Agree a time for discussion afterwards.

Setting criteria for observation and deciding on a format for lesson observation are useful activities for the whole department. You will end up with an agreed definition of good practice and a format for observing each other's lessons. This is a valuable means of active departmental training which need not be linked to appraisal.

It can be very difficult to find time to plan and carry out classroom observation. You may need to agree dates well in advance and put them forward as part of a departmental in-service training plan. The time involved is not just for the preparation and actual observation but also, and very importantly, for thoughtful feedback, discussion and target setting. When you give feedback to colleagues, remember that how you do it will affect how receptive they will be to your involvement and how useful the observation becomes.

Begin by asking them how they think the lesson went and ask them to identify the best aspects as well as those they would like to develop. Listen carefully and don't interrupt their analysis. Share things you noticed but which they may have missed. Ask your questions. Don't judge or criticise but help them to clarify their own opinions. Remember: it will be their turn to see you teach next!

Feeding back and planning forward

- Ask your colleague how they think the lesson went and develop this into a full discussion, listening carefully and being supportive.
- Record the strengths and areas for consideration.
- Discuss the priorities for development and the means to do so.

This completes the cycle – audit, plan, do and review. If you have developed any aspect of your classroom management, you have made an important step in helping your pupils towards the entitlement described by the National Curriculum. The cycle – audit, plan, do and review – represents a continuous process. The review stage brings you full circle to auditing and planning the next area for development. You may be working, for example, on one aspect of classroom management on your own or, alternatively, undertaking a full departmental review. If this seems difficult on occasions, remember that more effective classroom management will ensure more successful learning. Both you and your pupils will benefit!

Summary

- Be pleased with what you achieve and remember – it's a continuous process!

Booklist

Modern foreign languages for ages 11–16: Initial advice (National Curriculum Council, 1990)

Modern foreign languages in the National Curriculum (National Curriculum Council, 1991)

Non-statutory guidance (National Curriculum Council, 1992)

Teacher assessment at Key Stage 3 – Modern foreign languages (Secondary Examinations and Assessment Council, 1992)

The Modern Language Teacher's Handbook by Alan Smalley and David Morris (Stanley Thornes, 1992)

Equipping the modern languages classroom (National Association for Language Advisers, 1989)

Using the Target Language by Carol Macdonald (*Concepts* series, ALL/MGP 1993)

Appraisal for Language Teachers by Michael Pennington (*Concepts* series, ALL/MGP 1993)

Yes – but will they behave? Managing the interactive classroom by Susan Halliwell (Centre for Information on Language Teaching, 1991)

'Supporting teaching', article by Viv King in the series *The Practice Papers* (edited by Mary Newton) in *Special children* (1989)

Hands off – it's my go! IT in the languages classroom by Terry Atkinson (Centre for Information on Language Teaching, 1992)

Fair enough? Equal opportunities and modern languages by Vee Harris (Centre for Information on Language Teaching, 1992)

Miniflashcard Language Games by Susan Thomas and Frances Walsh (Miniflashcard Language Games, London, 1991)

You're not on your own!

Repromaster A
(see also repromaster B)

Who can I work with?

In school	**Details**
Head of department	______________________
Other colleagues in the department	______________________
	______________________
Pastoral staff	______________________
Mentor	______________________
SEN coordinator	______________________
IT coordinator	______________________
ESL teacher(s)	______________________
Assistant(s)	______________________
	______________________
Teachers of other subjects	______________________
	______________________
Librarian	______________________
Teacher in charge of audiovisual aids	______________________
Other(s)	______________________
	______________________

Out of school	**Details (including address and tel. no.)**
Inspector(s)	______________________
	______________________
	______________________
Advisory teacher(s)	______________________
	______________________
	______________________
Other(s)	______________________
	______________________

You're not on your own!

Repromaster B

(see also repromaster A)

Who can I work with?

Before drawing up details of your own support network, it might be helpful to read these notes.

In school, your **head of department** comes first as he or she should always know about the work of the languages team. Heads of department can seem perpetually busy, but if you make it clear that you need to talk about a classroom matter, they are often the best placed to help you.

Other colleagues within the department may also be able to help. Some departments have teachers in charge of a particular language, or with a designated responsibility. They are part of the internal support which a department offers.

The **pastoral** structure of a school offers support to all teachers when the concern is the child rather than that child's learning in a particular subject. Heads of department normally like to know when teachers seek advice from pastoral staff in case the matter has any departmental importance.

Newly qualified teachers work with an experienced teacher or a **mentor** who may be willing to offer advice on classroom management issues to any colleague.

The **Special Education Needs (SEN) coordinator**, and members of the SEN team, have much experience in assessing individual children's needs and drawing up personalised work programmes. They can offer valuable advice on differentiation and the planning strategies which underlie good classroom management. Some SEN colleagues may have responsibility for more able children and experience in setting up activities which will challenge them.

Don't forget the **Information Technology (IT) coordinator**. There may be only one computer in the department and yet we must ensure that pupils have a regular opportunity to 'use computers' (see *Programme of Study Part 1*). It may be possible to have access to a computer room for whole-class Information Technology/Modern Foreign Languages (IT/MFL) work, but the department must have a clear idea of how it is going to offer this opportunity to all pupils. References to IT should be in the scheme of work. The key to successful IT/MFL work is to know the potential learning outcomes of any software. In terms of classroom management, groupwork activities or independent work may be the most effective way of integrating IT. Clear ground rules should be established with the pupils. For example: How many pupils can work at the computer together? What is the time limit for computer work? How are decisions taken? What is our code of practice for working on computers?

Some schools have **teachers of English as a Second Language (ESL)**. These colleagues have a repertoire of language teaching techniques. They also have an understanding of how children acquire language which makes them valuable professional partners for foreign linguists.

Hopefully your school has a **foreign language assistant (FLA)**. Assistants come to the United Kingdom to work with teachers and their pupils, so make them part of your classroom rather than sending them away from it.

If you are developing a cross-curricular module, you will probably be working with a **teacher from another subject area**. Focus on the strengths and experience you both have: for example, the way in which a history teacher uses primary source materials may give you ideas on how to use authentic foreign language materials.

Finally, don't forget the **librarian** and the **teacher in charge of audiovisual aids**. Both have access to resources and a specialist understanding of how to make them work. The librarian will be able to help with reference material work. A technician may be able to video your lesson so that you can look at and appraise your own classroom management. Give these colleagues good warning if you would like their help as it is neither fair nor practical to rely on their availability.

There's a long list of **other people** who can help you in a school:

Can you bring sixth formers in to work with pupils on a carefully planned activity?

Can you prepare a lesson in which pupils gather information from exchange pupils?

Can you involve parents with foreign language skills?

Does the school have foreign language contacts in the local community or in local industries?

Can you organise a homework activity in which pupils interview staff? It's surprising how many teachers have the foreign language skills to answer questions from younger pupils but remember to warn staff and ensure that pupils prepare properly.

Out of school, if your local education authority has any languages staff, consultants or advisers perhaps, these may be able to offer support. There may be courses available, too, so ensure your head of department knows if you have an interest in classroom management.

Lesson plan proforma

Repromaster C

A completed proforma is on repromaster D.

(see also repromaster D)

Lesson Plan Proforma

Group: **Date:** **Time:**

Background:

Aim:

Preparation and resources needed:

Time	Activities	Opportunities for assessment (AT level)	*Programme of Study 1*

Homework:

Planned outcome:

Review of lesson: *(What were the strengths and weaknesses? Effect on future planning?)*

Lesson plan proforma

Repromaster D

(An example of detailed planning which encourages cross-referencing with the National Curriculum and so allows identification of next targets) *(see also repromaster C)*

Group: 8C **Date:** 23/3 **Time:** 2.10 - 3.20

Background: Last lesson, introduced T.V. programmes + channels.

Aim: To revise and practise giving information about expressing opinions on T.V. programmes by work in all skills, individually and in pairs.

Preparation and resources needed: "Communiquer" + tape OHT of prog. pictures T.V. mag. pages + OHT example Blank OHT grid H/W sheet OHT dialogue

Time	Activities	Opportunities for assessment (AT level)	*Programme of Study 1*
10 min	Revision of types of prog using OHT pictures e.g. Le film d'horreur, c'est quel numéro? L'émission numéro trois, qu'est-ce que c'est?		1, 7
	T/P → P/P Q/A work → Memory game: Ce soir je vais regarder...		69
5 min	Listening for gist: C'est quelle émission? "Communiquer" pp. 18 activ. 5	AT1, 3a	43
15 min	Authentic T.V. mag pages (including e.g. on OHT)		8
	a) Q/A on OHT Qu'est-ce que tu regardes ce soir?		51
	Sorte de prog? Chaîne? Commence/finit?		61
	b) Pair Q/A work based on real T.V. mag. pages		
15 min	Listening for details "Communiquer" p20 activ. 10 Check As orally + fill in on blank OHT grid.	AT1, 3b	44
15 min	Read dialogue on OHT (based on "Comm." p.20 activ. 11) → pair practice	AT2, 3b	5
	Listen to some e.g.s, rest of class note details		52
10 min	Write up dialogue.	Record marks	38

Homework: Differentiated worksheet: Letter re. T.V. + Qs. 49 51

Planned outcome:

Pupils have confidence + skills to describe T.V. programmes.

Review of lesson: *(What were the strengths and weaknesses? Effect on future planning?)*

+ Ps coped with listening activities well, probably because of thorough intro. of vocab. last lesson.
+ Ps interested in "real" pages from French T.V. mag.
- Ran out of time to prepare H/W sheet!

N.B. AT1, 3b Wai-Yee, Lorna, Robert, Chris, Angela
AT2, 3b Stuart, Steven, Wai-Yee, Lorna, Tracy, Billy

Designing activities

Repromaster E

(see also repromaster F)

1 Repetitive
Example:
Pairs are given three sets of cards (on different coloured card, if possible). Each set has visuals of one particular aspect of the topic – dates + times/activities/meeting places. Each pupil takes it in turns to take a card and give the French. If correct, the pupil keeps the card. Less able pupils may find it easier to practise with one set of cards at a time.

2 Closed
Example:
Cue cards to prompt conversation:

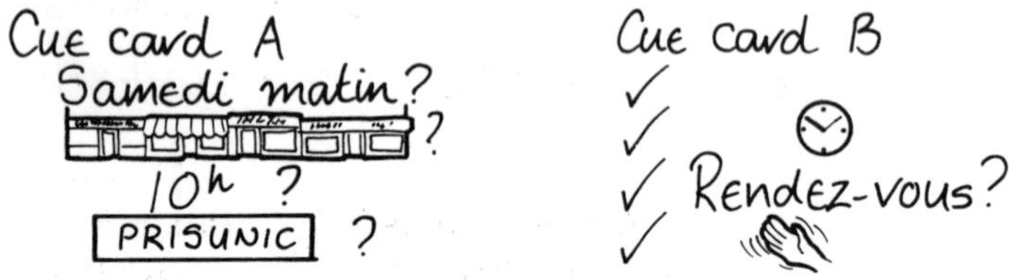

3 Information gap
Example:
Two identical street plans with × marked at bottom to indicate starting point:
Map A has symbols of cinema, café and sports centre marking their positions.
Map B has symbols of disco, post office and school marking their positions.

A: **Où est-ce qu'on se rencontre?**
B: **Au collège.**
A: **C'est où, le collège?**
B: **Prends la deuxième rue à gauche. Le collège est à droite.**

4 Open-ended
Example:

Vous avez cinq minutes. Combien d'activités pouvez-vous organiser pour le week-end prochain? Écrivez les détails sur cette fiche.

Activité?	Quand?	Rendez-vous

5 Unpredictable
Example:

A

Choisis une activité pour le week-end avec ton/ta partenaire.

B

Choisis une activité pour le week-end avec ton/ta partenaire.

AGENDA

Samedi : 10h café avec Pierre
18h télé : Les animaux d'Afrique
Dimanche : 9h messe
19h cinéma avec Sophie

♡ sport, musique pop

Designing activities

Repromaster F

(see also repromaster E)

6 Carousel

Example:

Organise class into groups – say, four groups of eight pupils.
Each group works in turn on one of four activities:
4 × 15 minutes

- Use simple *What's on* guide as a stimulus for 'Making a date' role-plays.
- Listen to 'Making a date' conversations on tape and note key information in grid.
- Use authentic materials (*What's on* information) to fill in blank diary for a week's holiday.
- Write a letter in the target language (on computer) asking someone for a date.

7 Drama

Example:

En groupe choisissez une activité pour le week-end. Chaque personne prend une carte ou un badge qui montre leur humeur.

Mood cards, for example:

de bonne humeur | de mauvaise humeur | enthousiaste | déprimé(e) | fatigué(e)

Badges on Velcro, for example:

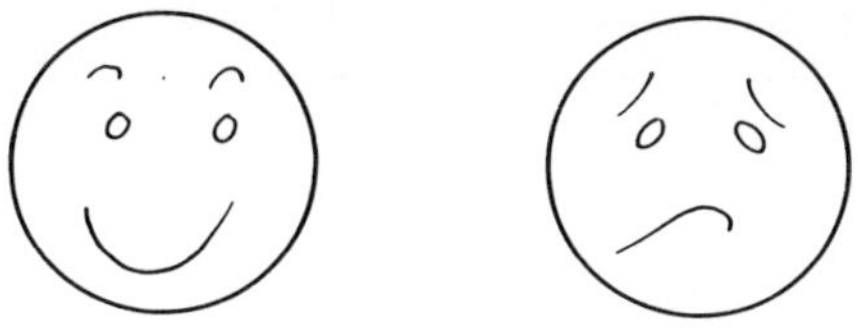

8 Problem-solving

Example:

Reading activity '**Qui peut sortir avec qui?**'
Pupils work together to solve clues (e.g. **Jean est libre samedi matin et dimanche soir. Sophie est libre tout le week-end. Sophie déteste faire du sport. Christophe aime aller au stade et au café…**) and match suitable pairs for a date.

9 Assignment

Example:

Pupils work in groups on task of setting up a Dating Agency. Possible activities include:

- Design an advert/poster for the agency.
- Prepare the recorded message for the agency answerphone.
- Design a proforma for clients to complete. (Create database?)
- Write a letter giving a client details of possible partners.
- Record telephone conversations of clients arranging dates together.
- Write letters/Record messages of thanks/complaint from clients.
- Act out (+video?) scene from date.

Organising groups

Repromaster G

Type of grouping	Type of activity	Appropriacy	Other comments
Example: Friendship	Speaking tasks at beginning of activity; homework tasks.	Supportive of pupils; motivational.	Ensure no one feels left out!

Summary of pupil evidence

Repromaster H

Modern Languages Department **19_____ – 19_____**

Summary of pupil evidence

Name: ______________________________ **Language:** ________________

Level one

AT	SoA	Date	Evidence
AT1 Listening	a) Understand and respond to familiar utterances of up to four words.	18 Sept	Follows simple classroom instructions.
	b) Identify individual items in a list.	25 Sept	Confident at pairwork on personal I.D.
AT2 Speaking	a) Respond briefly to what is seen or heard.	25 Sept	Confident at pairwork on personal I.D.
	b) Imitate with approximate pronunciation and intonation.	3 Oct	Accurate pronunciation of all pets in flashcard game.
AT3 Reading	a) Understand and respond to individual words presented in context.	6 Oct	Matched brief descriptions of people to picture cues.
AT4 Writing	a) Copy familiar words correctly.	12 Oct	Careful copying of family tree.

Pupil record card

Repromaster I

Modern Languages Department

MODERN FOREIGN LANGUAGES IN THE NATIONAL CURRICULUM

INDIVIDUAL PUPIL RECORD CARD

Name: ______________________

Date of birth: ____________

Language: ______________________

YEAR	7	8	9	10	11
TG					

[/] Attempted, not yet attained

[X] Attained

	LEVEL 1				LEVEL 2				LEVEL 3				LEVEL 4				LEVEL 5				LEVEL 6				LEVEL 7				LEVEL 8			
	a	b	c	d	a	b	c	d	a	b	c	d	a	b	c	d	a	b	c	d	a	b	c	d	a	b	c	d	a	b	c	d
AT1																																
AT2																																
AT3																																
AT4																																

	LEVEL 9				LEVEL 10			
	a	b	c	d	a	b	c	d
AT1								
AT2								
AT3								
AT4								

Comments/Targets

YEAR 7	
YEAR 8	
YEAR 9	
YEAR 10	
YEAR 11	

Sample of annotated piece of work — Repromaster J

(see Chapter 7)

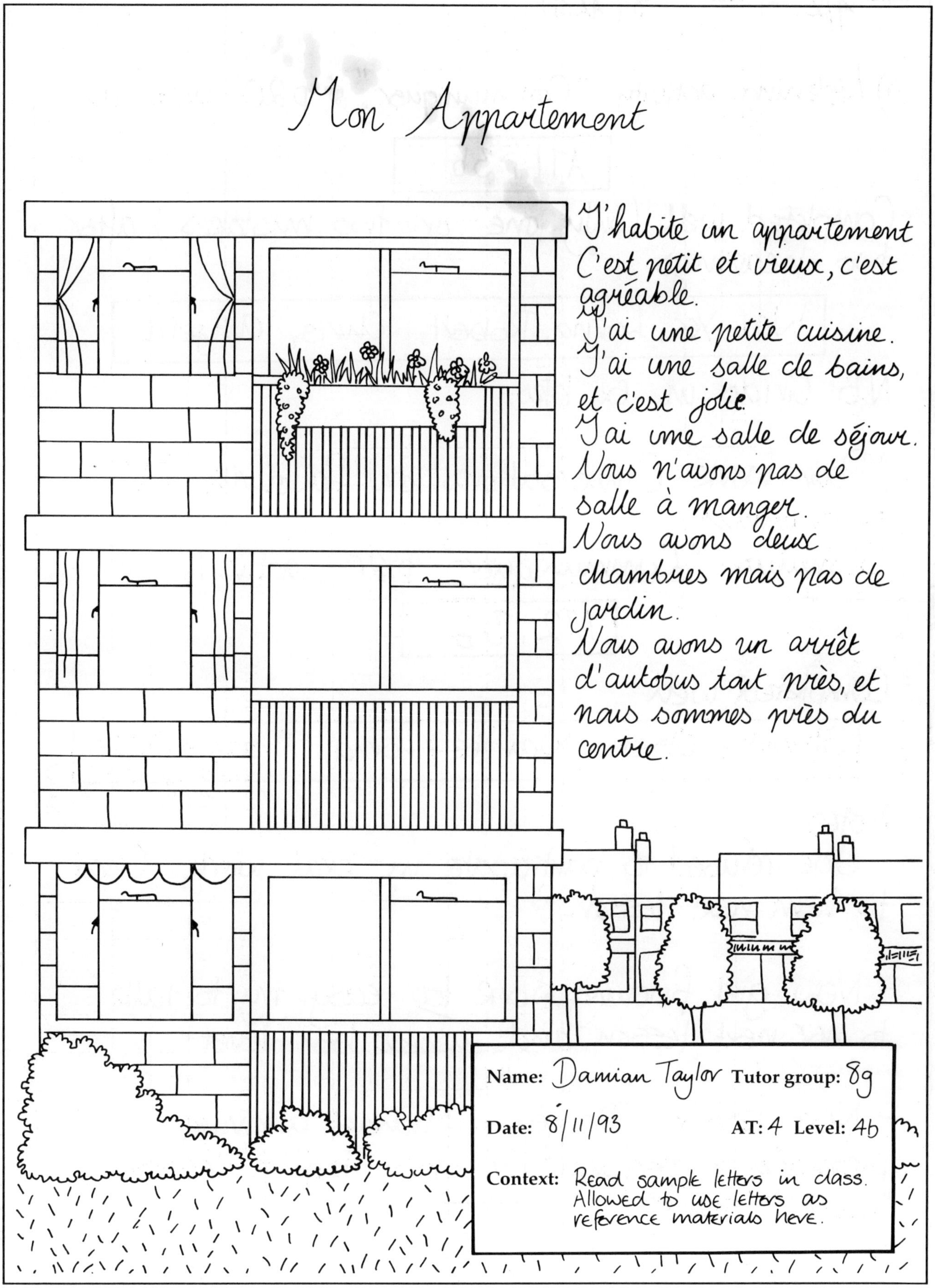

Teacher diary

Repromaster K

Date: 4/2 **Year:** 8 (ALG)

a) Listening activity "Communiquer" p.20 activ. 10

AT1, 3b

Completed well (only one or two mistakes) after two hearings:

Wai-Yee, Lorna, Robert, Chris, Angela

N.B. Grids in ex. bks.

b) Pair work. Conversations on favourite T.V. programmes.
Stimulus: "Communiquer" p.20 activ. 11

AT2, 3b

Completed well:

Stuart + Steven, Wai-Yee + Lorna, Tracy + Billy

Notes:
- Joe refused to participate in oral work. Chat to him next lesson?

- New girl finding work too easy - try to talk to her next lesson and assess her level.

- Next lesson: Darren + Michael arriving promptly to perform T.V. conv. before lesson "proper" starts.